Faith, Friendship & Focus

A 30 day devotional and workbook between friends.

By Rebekah Metteer

LAYOUT AND DESIGN BY SARA MARIE QUALLS

Published by Loving The Leap Ministries
© 2012 Rebekah Metteer
www.lovingtheleap.com

Designed by Sara Marie Qualls
sara.marie.qualls@gmail.com

No part of this book may be reproduced or transmitted in any form or by any means, electronic or mechanical, including photocopying and recording, or by an information storage or retrieval system, except as may be expressly permitted in writing by the publisher. Requests for permission should be addressed in writing to Loving The Leap Ministries; 7539 Douglas Ave S.E.; Snoqualmie, WA 98065.

ISBN: 978-0-615-62386-3

All scripture quotations, unless otherwise indicated, are taken from the Holy Bible, New International Version®, NIV®. Copyright ©1973, 1978, 1984, 2011 by Biblica, Inc.™ Used by permission of Zondervan. All rights reserved worldwide. www.zondervan.com

The "NIV" and "New International Version" are trademarks registered in the United States Patent and Trademark Office by Biblica, Inc.™

Printed in the United States of America.

DEDICATION

This book is devoted to Jesus who so lovingly spoke to my heart and placed in me the pursuit of His presence.

I also dedicate this to my husband Dan who has been my very best friend, my loving support, and my faithful prayer partner. Not a day goes by when I don't thank God for you in my life.

I dedicate this book to the women in my life who have encouraged me, lived life with me, and loved me for who I am. They are also the faithful women of God you see on the cover: Wendy Teh, Noelle Alvis, Sara Qualls, Deb Gerdes, Erin Julius, and Kelly Jester.

And to my mom, Valerie Vicknair, for being my greatest encourager and the woman I model my life after.

To my Dad, Richard Vicknair, who has served the Lord with such faithfulness and inspired my life to do the same.

Also to my amazing sister, Deborah Siers, who has walked with me through more life than anyone.

To my Pastors, friends, and family who have loved and prayed with me – I treasure you. Thank you all for serving Jesus with me. There's nothing better!

FOREWARD

When Rebekah Metteer told me that she was in the process of writing a devotional on faith, friendship, and focus, my heart cheered her on. It is an honor for me to tell you about Rebekah's heart and character. I have had the privilege of knowing her for many years and I can say that she is genuine and true to her faith in every way. She is a gifted speaker with a heart and desire to serve women.

This workbook was born because seven women decided to chase after God, and to encourage one another to go deeper with Christ. I anticipate that this devotional workbook is just the beginning of what God will bring from the season of growth and surrender that they chose to walk in together.

In the same way, I encourage you, as well as your friends, to take the thirty days recommended and forge a new place of faith and friendship. Trust God daily as you focus on the exercises you find within this workbook. Do not be discouraged if you miss something. Everyday is a new day; so choose today as your beginning. The journal portion of this workbook is critical for you to capture all that this experience has to offer. You will have recorded what God has spoken to you through this process. He will walk you through areas of repentance, sorrow, joy and thanksgiving.

I am grateful to Rebekah and her friends for being bold women, taking the time to invest in one another, and for the spirit of obedience that brought this to completion. I am praying that you find yourself meeting God in a new way and hearing the call to come near to Him just as they did.

With Great Expectancy,

Cheryl Jamison

INTRODUCTION

Welcome to your thirty day journey devotional and workbook! My hope is that you find a group of women to surround you as you begin this time of focus. Maybe it has been difficult to extend yourself to women, but no matter where you find yourself, I encourage you with all my heart to press into this adventure for all that God has for you. I believe the women the Lord is sending your way will support and help carry your burdens. Jesus wants to refresh your life and help push the reset button on your walk with Him. Accountability fuels motivation! That is why I encourage you to partner with women who can surround you. I know this journey will strengthen friendships and fuel your walk of faith. Together with accountability partners and friends, you will begin a time of focus on Jesus that affects your daily life. This will be thirty days of hard work that you will not regret. Refreshing revelation will come into the practical reality of your life as you welcome the Lord into every area.

Your first assignment begins with four specific chores that are accompanied by purposeful prayer. These chores are listed in the *Where to Start* section. Secondly, you will have the opportunity to strengthen the resolve of your spirit by giving up sugar or another stronghold for one month. A place to journal is provided to write down what the Lord is speaking to you. Thirdly, you will have the wonderful experience of sharing what God is doing in your life when meeting with your group of ladies weekly to go on a prayer walk together. Each day you will find a devotional, a focus word, and scripture to meditate on. After the thirty days are over, have a celebration dinner or dessert with your group. You will also share communion with the women who you have journeyed with.

At the end of these thirty days, I pray you will be renewed in your attitude toward your responsibilities and refreshed by His Word in your life. I know the Lord desires to lift you up and give you purpose. He wants to use your everyday life to produce a story and a testimony that will affect everyone around you. It's time to stop getting by and time to start living this great adventure called life. May you be blessed in your friendships, fueled in your faith, and determined in your focus. Jesus is waiting to walk out this journey with you.

Be Blessed!

Rebekah Metteer

WHERE TO START

Start by inviting a small group of friends to embark on this journey. Each lady should have their own workbook so they can journal and read the daily devotional.

Choose A Facilitator. Choose one person to be the facilitator of the group. There is a more detailed note to the facilitator on the following pages. Please take the time to read the section "*A Note To The Facilitator* if you are that person."

Get together to talk about how you need the Lord to refresh your life. There will be a total of four times that you will meet to walk and pray for one another within the thirty days. If you are meeting in the evening or during the winter months, you can gather for a time of prayer and worship in a home instead of walking outdoors. No matter where you meet, take the time to let down your guard. Share needs and words of encouragement with one another. Talk about the areas that you need to surrender to the Lord. Have your friends pray over you as you allow the Holy Spirit to come and bring freedom in the areas where you have been stuck. There is a place in this workbook to write down each other's prayer requests so that you can lift one another up during this journey.

Encourage each other to communicate outside of your weekly meeting. You can e-mail, or better yet, send one another cards in the mail. Even just one received card might be the very thing which lifts another woman out of her rut.

For thirty days give up sugar. This is a way of allowing the Lord to strengthen your inner spirit and help deny the will of your flesh. Consider it a sugar fast. Ask the Lord to strengthen your resolve so that even your will comes into alignment with His purpose for your life. This is not a diet but rather a spiritual discipline that you will reap many benefits from. If giving up sugar seems trivial for you, feel free to pray and ask the Lord what else He might want you to give up in order to deny your flesh and strengthen your spirit. It might be giving up your favorite television show for that month, or giving up specific free time to spend in God's Word.

WHERE TO START

Take part in the four prayer tasks/chores each day. Every day, for thirty days, you will do four specific chores that are accompanied by specific prayers spoken over yourself and your family. Try your best to do them all in order to reap the full benefits of what the Lord wants to speak and do in your life. Just remember—you can do anything for thirty days!

Here are your four prayer tasks/chores:

- *Make your bed each morning and pray for your spouse or over your future.* Pray for the Lord to minister to your husband and to draw you closer to one another. Do your best to do this every day. *If you are single*, while making your bed, pray for purity, contentment, and whatever God's will is for you in this area of life.

- *Wash a load of laundry everyday.* As you do this, ask the Lord to do some "laundry" in your own life. Ask Him to reveal the areas where you need to surrender. Be listening throughout the day as the Lord speaks to your spirit about things that might need to be cleansed in your life.

- *Fold the laundry for the day and put it away for each person.* As you go through the act of putting away each person's items, ask the Lord to take control of their individual lives. In other words, lay your family members before the Lord. Pray specifically over each child, your spouse, and even over your own life. Ask the Lord to direct them, speak to them, guide them and use their lives to bring Him glory. Try to put at least one thing away on their behalf each day. *If you are single or an empty-nester*, ask the Lord to help you lay your life down for His calling. Surrender to Him your hopes, dreams, and even your identity. Ask Him to give you an identity that is sure and strong in Him alone.

- *Put away the dishes each day.* As you put them away in their rightful places, ask the Lord to help reprioritize your life. Ask Him to show you where your time belongs. Ask Him to organize your thoughts and strengthen your prayer life as you seek His will.

*Note about the prayer tasks/chores: If any of these chores are the responsibility of another member in your household, either give them a month off, or share the duty with them. But I encourage you to make the most out of each one of these tasks so you and your family can reap maximum benefits in the spiritual realm.

WHERE TO START

Each day in your workbook you will find a new focus word. Read the coinciding devotional and allow the Lord to speak into your life about that topic. You may even want to write the scripture and focus word for the day on a sticky note and put it on your refrigerator or on the dashboard of your car. Pray for the Lord to do a new work in your heart each day. You will also find a scripture to focus on. Read it or even try to memorize a few of them to help you renew your mind.

At the end of your journey together, plan a celebration dinner or dessert! Host it at someone's house. Take turns sharing what the Lord has done in your life over the past thirty days. Then take communion together at the end of the dinner. Ask the Lord to give you a fresh perspective on His calling in your life and begin to walk out your new freedom.

TASKS IN A NUTSHELL

These are your tasks in a nutshell:

1. Gather a small group and make sure everyone has a book.

2. Choose a facilitator.

3. Plan a day each week to go for a prayer walk together or to meet for prayer in someone's home.

4. Read your daily devotion and journal what the Lord is speaking to you. Focus on the word and scripture of the day. Talk with your accountability group each week about how those words impact your life.

5. Complete your "prayer tasks/chores" each day with the purpose of asking the Lord to come and do a work in your life and in the life of your family. If you are unsure what the chores are, see "the four daily chores" list on the previous page.

6. Give up sugar or another desire of the flesh.

7. Encourage one another through phone, e-mail, text, and/or cards.

8. Have a celebration dinner or dessert at the end of the thirty days. Break your sugar fast and take communion together. Share your thirty day story of how God has reset your focus.

*Although these tasks/chores will benefit you greatly, the goal is not simply to check them off the list. This journey is all about pursuing Jesus in everything that you do. Do your best, but if you miss a task, there is no condemnation in Christ Jesus.

A NOTE TO THE FACILITATOR

I feel blessed to partner with you in ministering to women! If you are the facilitator of your group then you are the one encouraging your ladies to press into the Lord for these thirty days in order to see what God will do. I urge you to pray for the women that are already in your small circle or for those who you have yet to invite.

As a facilitator, you should be the one to send out e-mails to your group encouraging them in their thirty day pursuit. Sometimes it is easy to give up, but with accountability the perseverance gets easier.

When you first meet with the women in your group, set up a weekly time for the prayer walk or prayer gathering. As a leader, try your very best to be at all of the prayer meetings. If the group is spread apart in distance and a prayer and fellowship time is difficult to accomplish, one can experience the prayer walk with the Lord on their own and still benefit. If distance is an issue and one of the group members chooses to do the prayer walk on their own, please make sure to communicate with that person through some other avenue.

Each week, encourage the ladies to share what the Lord is speaking to them personally. Be sensitive to the fact that someone might share very personal information. Let your group know that any personal information that is shared is to be treasured and protected. Try to focus while you walk and keep your conversation about the Lord and what he is doing in the lives of those in the group. Ask questions of each woman so everyone has a chance to share what is going on in their lives. When you close in prayer, encourage the women to keep their requests focused on their personal journey with the Lord. Let this be a time for these women to be refreshed by the presence of God.

Each day the ladies will have an opportunity to journal what the Lord has spoken to them. There is a journal page at the end of each devotional. Encourage your group to read the devotion for the day in the morning and then journal a short prayer or thought at night. This will really add to their thirty day journey. It is so important to keep the focus on seeking Jesus and not to get caught up in just checking off the chore list for the day. The chores are intended to be a physical representation of what the Lord is doing in our spirits.

A NOTE TO THE FACILITATOR

Encourage the women in your group to embrace the full spectrum of this journey. This includes the prayer tasks and chores, the reading of daily devotions and journal, the giving up of sugar, the prayer walks, and the celebration dinner and communion. If someone in your group has already given up sugar for health reasons, encourage them to give up something else in their pursuit of giving up the "junk." This way the Lord can have their full attention. It may be giving up a television show, bread, or even giving up sleeping-in so they have time to seek the Lord aside from their normal routine.

When your group finishes the thirty days of focus, you will want to ask someone to host a celebration dinner or dessert. You are welcome to host it yourself, but it is always fun to have someone else contribute to the experience. You, as a leader, will want to bring communion to your celebration dinner. The dinner can be fancy or casual, but it should carry with it a time of meaningful reflection of what the Lord has done in all of your lives. Tell the ladies to be prepared to bring their workbooks and to share from them what God is speaking in their lives.

At the end of the dinner take communion together. Grape juice and crackers or bread will work just fine for this purpose. Thank the Lord for His forgiveness, grace, and redemption. Ask Him to reset your life on a path of total focus on Jesus. You will find the scripture on communion in *1 Corinthians 11:23-29*. You can read this scripture aloud, then drink the juice and take the bread upon reflection of the Lord's forgiveness. If there are ladies in your group who have not yet asked Jesus to come and be the leader of their life, this is a great time to pray for them to receive Christ before partaking in communion.

In the back of the work book you will find a thirty day calendar that you might want to use during your first gathering. This will help you decide which day to meet for your prayer walk or prayer gathering. There are few pages for prayer requests as well.

Take the time to write down each other's phone numbers, e-mails, and mailing addresses. This will help you stay connected. Try your best to stay in touch with your ladies by phone or letter instead of just by e-mail. Adding that personal touch will make all the difference in furthering your friendship. There is a place to record this information in the back of the workbook.

A NOTE TO THE FACILITATOR

I am so proud of you as a leader. You don't have to be anything other than who you already are. You are loved, you are called, and you are making a difference with your encouragement in the lives of these women. Remember, each life changed, each life reset, each life refocused affects an entire family.

Take the Leap!

FAITH, FRIENDSHIP & FOCUS

Day 1	Expectation
Day 2	Focus
Day 3	Vision
Day 4	Priorities
Day 5	Service
Day 6	Joy
Day 7	Agenda
Day 8	Renew
Day 9	Cleanse
Day 10	Passion
Day 11	Identity
Day 12	Worth
Day 13	Love
Day 14	Pursuit
Day 15	Insecurity
Day 16	Humility
Day 17	Purpose
Day 18	Strength
Day 19	Perseverance
Day 20	Waiting
Day 21	Calling
Day 22	Belief
Day 23	Trust
Day 24	Anger
Day 25	Loneliness
Day 26	Holiness
Day 27	Fear
Day 28	Gratitude
Day 29	Change
Day 30	Praise

Day 1

EXPECTATION

The devotional portion, which you are about to begin, is only one part of what you will participate in during this thirty day journey. If you have not already done so, take time to read the "Where to Start" section as it will explain all other daily activities involved with this study.

As you start this day, ask the Lord to prepare you to receive all that He has for you. Ask Him to make this journey a life-altering pursuit. Open your heart to all that He has for you. Lay down your own expectations and let the Lord push the reset button in your life.

As individuals we set high hopes for how our day, or life for that matter, will turn out. Many times we even try to manipulate our surroundings so that we will not be disappointed by the high expectations we have made. *Expectation* is the first focus word in your thirty day journey.

We place high expectation on ourselves as well as others. Consider who your expectation rests upon. Who do you expect to be responsible for your circumstances? Who do you expect to be responsible for your life? Is it you? Is it another person? Is it your Creator God? We have an open invitation to go to the Lord and allow Him to take control. Instead of your expectations resting upon your own shoulders, our personal and powerful God wants us to expect that He can do the impossible for us. When we go to Him with our day, with our time, and with our relationships, He will take control. He will wow us with His ability to meet and exceed our expectations. We can expect that God will provide an outcome far better than we could ever have achieved in our own strength.

Ask yourself these questions: What do I expect of myself? What do I expect of others? What do I expect of my God? Often, we attempt to meet our own expectations. We do not want to bother anyone else with our issues, so we take on the role of super woman, self-counselor, and problem solver. All of the expectation falls on our own shoulders. Then, when we fail, we turn and place our expectations on others. We become needy and insecure. Because people are flawed, they will never meet our expectations one hundred percent of the time. Our lack of communication and unrealistic expectation of others leave us disappointed, hurt, and bitter. When we have exhausted others and ourselves, we finally turn in broken expectation to the Lord. We go to Him for answers, but because of past disappointment, we come with a certain amount of distrust in God's ability. The Lord longs

EXPECTATION

for you to come to Him first so that you no longer rely on the flawed, painful cycle that comes when we strive to meet our own expectations.

When we associate the word "expectation" with the name of the Lord, the two combine to create an immovable, unchangeable truth about His character. He is flawless in His love for you. He is perfect in His plan over your life. His promises are sure. Our expectancy of God can be solid and absolute. We have the ability to have expectations that hope, believe and press into the things of God because we know who He is. He cannot, nor will He ever, let us down. For in His Word He declares, "Never will I forsake you" (Hebrews 13:5b). It is against the character of God to let you down. Only your misplaced expectations can let you down.

Today, join me in asking the Lord to fix the placement of our expectations. Let's specifically ask Jesus to reverse the order in which we function. In this new order, we first go to the Lord with a certain and sure trust in how He can help, heal, and renew. We see ourselves in the light of His ability and not our own. Our outlook then becomes one of obedience to God instead of discouragement from our weakness.

As we listen to and obey the voice of the Lord, any expectation to measure up or have others meet our needs, turns into a desire to bring every relationship and situation to the Lord.

Ask the Lord to help you rely on Him more fully. Ask for help in putting your expectations in His ability rather than your own. He designed us to rely on Him.

Expectation:
"When we associate the word "expectation" with the name of the Lord, the two combine to create an immovable, unchangeable truth about His character. He is flawless in His love for you. He is perfect in His plan over your life. His promises are sure."

"The Lord is my strength and shield; my heart trusts in Him and I am helped. My heart leaps for joy and I will give thanks to Him in song." Psalm 28:7

JOURNAL - DAY ONE

Day 2

FOCUS

The Lord designed us to put Him in our focus each day. When we start our day with Jesus as our focus, our mind, our attitude, and our spiritual hearing are dialed into Him as well. When you focus on Jesus, the entrapments that the enemy has set (insecurities, anger, or frustration) must come under the control of the Lord. It no longer has the power that the enemy intended.

Sometimes we feel too overwhelmed or hurried to simply sit and be with Jesus. However, focus is not necessarily about being on our knees in a quiet room or getting alone with God to study His Word. It is also learning how to think on the Lord throughout the day. Your daily chores combined with prayer will accomplish more than you may realize. By day two, you may not be feeling very "spiritual" at all. It may seem like thirty days of focus are going to be more work than you want to do. But I assure you, that as you go through the practice of letting the Lord permeate even the mundane chores of your day, you are retraining your focus to be set on the Lord.

Focus makes a difference! Rather than putting clothes away and feeling a sense of resentment because you are doing housework alone, you are instead praying God's blessing over your life and the lives of those in your family. Your spirit is being trained to care about things that matter. Instead of feeling worn-out and under-appreciated, your heart and mind are in tune to the good purposes of God for your life.

Focusing our spirit is not something we need to try and do once in a while. Rather, we need to mature our spirit by teaching it to dwell in the presence of the Lord all day long. The Psalmist knew the importance of this when he said, "Guide me in Your truth and teach me, for You are God my Savior, and my hope is in You all day long" (Psalm 25:5). By keeping your every minute awareness on the presence of Jesus, you are silencing the lies of the enemy.

Isaiah 26:3 speaks of our God keeping you in perfect peace if your mind is steadfast in Him. What would it look like for you to keep your mind, your thoughts, and your emotions steadfast on the Lord? Would your reactions change when life gets frustrating? Would you pay attention to the neighbor who so desperately needs Jesus? Would it change the way you interact with your spouse? Jesus changes us. When our focus is on Him, we are able to open our hands and accept *His* plan, *His* correction, and *His* compassion.

As you are praying through your chores, ask the Lord to mature your focus. Pray that your heart, your mind, and your spirit would think upon the things of God so that you will be ready when life comes to frustrate you.

Focus:
"Focus is not necessarily about being on our knees in a quiet room or getting alone with God to study His Word. It is also learning how to think on the Lord throughout the day."

"You will keep in perfect peace those whose minds are steadfast because they trust in You."
Isaiah 26:3

JOURNAL - DAY TWO

Day 3

VISION

When we have vision for the future, we see beyond our present circumstances to something that is yet to come. Do you have a vision of what God wants to do with your future? Can you imagine that the Lord is working in you today so that He can use your life to testify of His goodness tomorrow?

How many times have you heard the phrase, "seeing is believing?" In times of uncertainty, we like to have proof in order to accept that something is fact. The Lord is daily giving you proof as to what He can do in your life. He walks you through trouble and brings you through to victory on the other side. He is using your current situations and struggles to produce a woman with a story; a woman who can prove by her testimony that Jesus can change any circumstance. When you ask God for vision, He gives you the ability to appreciate that your everyday life can produce a dynamic story an amazing testimony of God's provision, strength, and goodness. Vision sees the "healed-you" in the midst of the "broken-you". Vision also gives you the desire to tell your story after God's healing and provision have come. When you glorify God by sharing all that He has done, you are living your life to the fullest and His vision for your life is being fulfilled.

Proverbs 29:18 says, "Where there is no vision, the people perish" (KJV). What if this scripture read a little more personally: "If (your name) doesn't have a vision for her future, she will perish." Without vision you will live a life feeling like everything you do is meaningless. You will continually feel like you do not measure up. Without a vision, you will live day after day feeling unsatisfied, unmotivated, even unloved, and may eventually give up. Vision motivates you to use your circumstances as stepping stones, teaching tools, and an opportunity to testify of God's grace. Having a vision for where the Lord is preparing you to go and what He is preparing you to do will bring encouragement to your soul.

If it has been a while since you have had a vision for your life and future, then ask the Lord to give it to you. The Lord wants to open the eyes of your heart. He wants to show you how He is using your life today for what He will accomplish tomorrow. You may know right away the vision that the Lord is revealing concerning your future, or you may have no idea. One thing is for sure, the Lord's vision for your life includes you sharing your daily life victories with others, so start there.

VISION

Today, write down some of the hard areas in your life that you are dealing with. Write down the ways that the Lord could be using those situations to change you, to train you, and to shape you. Then, in accordance with God's character and promises, write down what your testimony might be after you have come out on the other side. What might you be able to share with a friend about a time when your marriage was struggling? Is there a story of God's healing you will be able to share with others? What might you be able to testify on moments of victory where the Lord led you out of a difficult place?

When you can measure your current life with the faithfulness and promises of God, then you have vision. Vision says, "Lord I know who You are. I know You are working in me. I know You love me and that You are pouring out Your righteousness in me. I can see how You are preparing greater things. I can see a vision of myself testifying of Your goodness." Get up in the morning looking forward to hearing His voice. He wants to use your life to bring glory and honor to the name of Jesus. The Lord has a vision of you serving Him that has great purpose and significance. You are becoming the person He wants you to be!

As you go about your day, ask the Lord to give you a vision for your future. Look to Him for revived motivation.

***Vision*:**
"He is using your current situations and struggles to produce a woman with a story, a woman who can prove by her testimony that Jesus can change any circumstance. When you ask God for vision, He gives you the ability to appreciate that your everyday life can produce a dynamic story, an amazing testimony of God's provision, strength, and goodness. Vision sees the "healed-you" in the midst of the "broken-you".

"There is surely a future hope for you, and your hope will not be cut off." Proverbs 23:18

JOURNAL - DAY THREE

Day 4

PRIORITIES

There are many things we count as priorities, like getting our house clean, running errands, exercise, and maybe even a nap if you are lucky. Yet, few of these priorities actually serve to benefit your inner person. For example, exercise will certainly strengthen your outer person, but without strengthening your inner person, even being physically fit will come up empty in the end.

There is nothing like being with Jesus to benefit your inner person. He fills you with joy. He comforts your sorrow. He calms anxiety and listens to your needs. When our relationship with Jesus is our number one priority, every other priority falls under His direction, strength, and authority. We are able to relinquish control when we put Jesus in His rightful place as the head and leader of our lives.

When something in your life is treated with more importance than another thing, it has become your priority. Then, whether you like it or not, those priorities demand the right to come before everything else. There are few things in life that should actually have the right to come first. According to God's Word there are certain things that hold this right. One is to "Love the Lord your God with all your heart, and with all your soul, and with all your strength" (Deuteronomy 6:5). Another is teaching your family the things of God. "Talk about them when you sit at home and when you walk along the road, when you lie down and when you get up" (Deuteronomy 6:7). Love for the Lord and love of your family are two things that deserve our utmost attention.

When we place the Lord as the number one priority in our lives we reap huge benefits. Our attitude is corrected. Anxiety and fear are dispelled. Bitterness and resentment are brought to light. Life does not stop when you put Jesus as a priority. In fact, it is just beginning. He wants to show how He can be victorious in the midst of your circumstances. He wants to take you on an adventure of a lifetime!

Then He wants you to praise Him. Praise produces a testimony that must be told. That is where the adventure begins. Your family, your friends, and even strangers are waiting for you to show them what Jesus has done for you on a personal level. So, wake up in the morning with Jesus on your mind and hearing His voice as your most important priority. He will give you the ability to recognize His voice throughout your day. The Lord is ready for you to surrender your old ways and to put Him before everything else. He holds the right to be your number one, and He will astound you!

Ask the Lord to help your heart and mind acknowledge Him as your most important priority. Ask Him to show you the areas of your life that need to be re-prioritized as you meditate on His Word.

Priorities:
"When we put our relationship with Jesus as our number one priority, every other situation falls under His direction, His strength, and His authority."

"I am the Lord, and there is no other; apart from me there is no God. I will strengthen you, though you have not acknowledged me, so that from the rising of the sun to the place of its setting men may know there is none besides me. I am the Lord, and there is no other." Isaiah 45:5-6

JOURNAL - DAY FOUR

Day 5

SERVICE

When our eyes are open to see all of the amazing things our God is doing here and around the world, our hearts are moved to be a part of it. It is human nature to want to be where the party is! We love to be invited to the big event. People will sign up to serve at a multitude of events when they feel like it matters. Well, the Lord is inviting you to serve at His big event.

At times, we view service as something we are forced to do for the Lord out of duty. We see servants as humble, meek people who have given up everything in life simply to be devoted to God. However, if we understood that service is actually an invitation from the Lord asking us to be a part of a mighty work He has planned, we would be all in and honored to be there!

When God invites you to serve Him, He is providing an opportunity to enrich your life with significant meaning. You can serve a lot of things and a lot of people that will take advantage of you, but the Lord will actually give you the advantage when you walk in His service. At times, I find it hard to remember that I have been invited to God's big event. Most of the time I am just at home doing chores and cleaning up behind the family. I do not feel like a servant but more of a slave to daily duties. I now realize that this perpetual home life has actually become my training ground to build up my character. It is in my everyday normal life that it becomes obvious if my attitude lacks the fruit of the Spirit. The Lord is equipping me as I seek Him in my home to go out from there and be effective.

Every day during this thirty day journey you will pray over your family. You may never know the difference that your prayers make. As you sow seeds on a daily basis over your spouse, your family, and over your own future, God is hearing every word. You may be the only one praying over your loved ones, but those prayers move the heart of God and alter the circumstances of your life and those you are praying for. Daily prayer matters.

Sign your heart up for service and rejoice in the fact that you are invited to God's big event. He has something in the works that will blow your mind!

Ask the Lord to show you how He wants you to serve Him today. Rejoice that you are a part of something big, even while you live out your daily life obeying Him.

***Service*:**
"When God invites you to serve Him, He is providing an opportunity to enrich your life with significant meaning. You can serve a lot of things and a lot of people that will take advantage of you, but the Lord will actually give you the advantage when you walk in His service."

"Serve wholeheartedly, as if you were serving the Lord, not men." Ephesians 6:7

JOURNAL - DAY FIVE

JOY

Joy is a complex word because it is not necessarily defined as happiness. Nor is it always accompanied by laughter. These things can come along with joy, but do not define it. Happiness is controlled by our own state of mind and roller coaster of emotions, whereas joy is derived when something external satisfies you. The only external source that will truly fulfill you is the Lord. 1 Chronicles 16:27 says, "Splendor and majesty are before Him; strength and joy in His dwelling place." You will find your joy again when you find yourself in the dwelling place of God. This is the only place where you will be satisfied. This world has nothing for you. When the Lord becomes the focus, we stop relying on our own strength to supply joy. Joy comes by knowing Christ. He is exceptionally good. He is exceptionally satisfying. He is a continual, never-ending starting place for joy.

If we place our expectations on the Lord and His character, we will experience a joy like we have never known. A joy that satisfies even when life is difficult. A joy that motivates even when our own insecurity wants to keep us from moving forward. A joy that happens to us because we have been in the presence of the Lord. Joy comes from knowing the character of God and believing that He is working on our behalf.

Jesus said, "As the Father has loved me, so I have loved you. Now remain in My love. If you obey My commands, you will remain in My love, just as I have obeyed My Father's commands, and remain in His love. I have told you this so that My joy may be in you and that your joy may be complete" (John 15:9-11). It is God's good desire for your life to be filled with joy. It comes when we go to Jesus and hear from Him.

Has your life been lacking joy? Perhaps the Lord is calling you back to a place of hearing His voice and being in His presence. Romans 10:17 says, "Faith comes from hearing the message, and the message is heard through the word of Christ." The Lord is prompting us to come! Come and be filled by Him. Be filled by studying God's words over your life. Come and receive His fullness. He is the source of a never-ending fountain of joy, and that fountain is for you to drink from. Hurry to His presence. He has a gift for you.

Let's get back to the art of listening to His voice. Today, find some time to look in the back of your Bible at the word joy. Choose three or more scriptures to look up and journal about. What does the Bible say about joy? Pray those scriptures over your life. How does the Lord want to satisfy your need and fill you with hope?

Joy:
"If we place our expectations on the Lord and His character, we will experience a joy like we have never known. A joy that satisfies even when life is difficult. A joy that motivates even when our own insecurity wants to keep us from moving forward. A joy that happens to us because we have been in the presence of the Lord."

"Splendor and majesty are before Him; strength and joy in His dwelling place." 1 Chronicles 16:27

JOURNAL - DAY SIX

Day 7

AGENDA

Each day brings a new set of responsibilities—things we want to accomplish and things we want to get done. With so many things to do we can be forced to live life with a sense of dissatisfaction called "if only". If only we had more time. If only we could have a moment to ourselves. If only everyone were not so messy. If only I had more money. The list goes on and on. When the "if only" meets with our current agenda, our ability to accomplish anything is dramatically reduced. We are left trying to overcome all the "if only's" in order to fulfill our agenda. We own the day. Though, in the end, all we feel is empty, deprived, and unproductive. When the agenda belongs to us, it carries with it an enormous amount of disappointment if it cannot be accomplished. The disappointment can lead to anger, frustration, arguments, and immense dissatisfaction.

On the other hand, what if we woke up each morning and gave our agenda to the Lord? Perhaps He would rearrange it just a bit and help us with the things that matter. The Lord is interested in your day. He wants peace and joy for your life instead of chaos, un-fulfillment, and a bucket of "if only's". He wants to own the day. Oh, the headaches we would avoid if we would start the day by giving our agenda up to God!

God is omniscient. His wisdom is dependable. If you could see your life as God sees it—beginning, middle, and end—your agenda would inevitably change. So what is holding you back from releasing your agenda? Are you afraid that God will take away the things you long to do?

Give your wishes, your desires, and tasks to the Lord, and what He gives you in exchange will be filled with more purpose, more satisfaction, and more meaning than before. It is foolish to try to make it through your day without asking the One who knows the outcome. The Lord has the ability to move mountains on your behalf and help you accomplish anything. You just have to ask. Either trust your own agenda and all that it will bring, or trust God's agenda and see what He will bring.

Today, instead of hitting the ground running with your agenda leading the way, ask the Lord to re-prioritize your day. He will speak to you and give you divine wisdom.

Agenda:
"Either trust your own agenda and all that it will bring, or trust God's agenda and see what He will bring."

"Humble yourselves, therefore, under God's mighty hand, that He may lift you up in due time. Cast all your anxiety on Him because He cares for you." 1 Peter 5:6-7

JOURNAL - DAY SEVEN

Day 8

RENEW

"Do not conform any longer to the patterns of this world, but be transformed by the renewing of your mind. Then you will be able to test and approve what God's will is—His good, pleasing and perfect will" (Romans 12:2). Today you might be feeling weary, as you contemplate the days you have finished. It is day eight and you have passed the one week mark! You are well on your way to deepening your hunger for Christ as you allow Him to permeate your daily life.

Romans 12:2 talks about not conforming any longer to your old patterns. We have created multiple patterns in our lives, many of which are destructive. The Lord wants to get us out of that rut. Through this journey, you are creating new patterns of seeking God in the daily routine. You are choosing to strengthen your spirit and deny your flesh. You are reaching out in friendship and the Lord is rewarding you with something more meaningful than you had before. Today is a day to rejoice and be renewed.

To be renewed is to start again after a time of interruption. What is interrupting your life? Renewing yourself, your mind, and your relationship with God can bring fresh passion and strength. It is time to reestablish your relationship with the Lord. There are so many distractions in this life, and we have been interrupted for far too long. The Lord wants to get our attention. He wants to change our bad habits and our old patterns.

It is possible for you to have a fresh start in pursuit and in purpose. You don't have to wait until tomorrow for the Lord to renew you. Repent today. Turn from your old ways and walk in liberty. Strengthen your spirit. You are allowing God to restore your mind as you do your daily chores, pray with purpose, and keep your focus on the Lord. He will create patterns that will produce self-control, patience, peace, joy, love, and every fruit of the Spirit. Jesus wants to renew your determination today. You can do it!

Pray that the Lord would renew your motivation to seek Him. Ask Him to strengthen your resolve to obey Him and to listen to His voice. The Lord desires to renew you completely. Connect with an accountability partner today and encourage one another to stick with it! Be steadfast!

Renew:
"There are so many distractions in this life, and we have been interrupted for far too long! The Lord wants to get our attention. He wants to change our bad habits and our old patterns. It is His desire that we do just as Romans 12:2 says, "Do not conform any longer to the pattern of this world, but be transformed by the renewing of your mind. Then you will be able to test and approve what God's will is—His good, pleasing, and perfect will.""

"Therefore we do not lose heart. Though outwardly we are wasting away, yet inwardly we are being renewed day by day." 2 Corinthians 4:16

JOURNAL - DAY EIGHT

Day 9

CLEANSE

"Surely you, [Lord], desire truth in the inner parts; You teach me wisdom in the inmost place. Cleanse me with hyssop and I will be clean; wash me, and I will be whiter than snow" (Psalm 51:6-7). Do you need to be cleansed from pride, lust, insecurity, anger, or self-pity? Do you need the Lord to tear down the walls you have put up in your life? Have you been plagued with a self-reliance that is pushing the Lord to a lesser place? It is to your benefit that you allow Christ to be the Lord of every area of your life. He took His place upon the cross so that you could be free from sin. Without the cleansing of Christ, we are lost.

What are some of the deep places in your life that the Lord desires to purify? As you have been going through the act of doing laundry each day and praying about the Lord doing a deeper cleansing in your life, what has been coming to the surface? Psalm 51:6-7 talks about being cleansed with "hyssop". In biblical times, hyssop was used not only to cleanse the body, but also to cleanse and purify temples and sacred places. So, when the Bible says "cleanse me with hyssop and I will be clean" it means that Jesus is the purifier and you are His temple, His sacred place.

The Bible says, "For we are the temple of the living God" (2 Corinthians 6:16b). Your life is a sacred place where the Lord is dwelling. He desires to cleanse you in every secret place so that you can live purely and effectively. He desires truth to be seen even in your inner being. He is waiting to speak to you and give you wisdom about why you struggle with the things you do. He wants to tell you where the enemy has been lying to you. He wants to show you how to move forward from the entrapments you have been living in.

Yesterday, we talked about being renewed and starting afresh. I find it fitting for us to take one step deeper and ask the Lord to do some house cleaning within. Ask Him to speak to you about what He desires to cleanse in your life. Ask Him to purify your thoughts, your intentions, and your attitude as you worship him through your daily activities. Repentance sets you free from a cycle of destruction. Freedom awaits!

Find some time today to ask the Lord to show you the areas in your life that need His cleansing. Sin is destructive, but repentance brings freedom.

Cleanse:
"Your life is a sacred place where the Lord is dwelling. He desires to cleanse you in every secret place so that you can live purely and effectively. He desires truth to be seen even in your inner being. He is waiting to speak to you and give you wisdom about why you struggle with the things you do. He wants to tell you where the enemy has been lying to you. He wants to show you how to move forward from the entrapments you have been living in."

"He who has clean hands and a pure heart, who does not lift up his soul to an idol or swear by what is false. He will receive blessing from the Lord." Psalm 24:4-5a

JOURNAL - DAY NINE

Day 10

PASSION

Is there something you are passionate about? Is it cooking, or exercise, or decorating? Maybe you are passionate about a concept, thought, or idea. Perhaps you are in a season of life where passion seems like something from a distant place in your youth. Passion is caused by a strong emotion about something. When you are passionate about a certain topic, it stirs up an emotion in you that causes you to care, to act, or to share about that thing.

How would life change if you were passionate about seeking and knowing God? Would you act differently? Would you care more about people? Would some of your current passions lessen because of your passion for Christ? Would you share from your heart more often? When you invest your heart, your life, and your emotion into something, it changes the way you act. The more time you spend throughout your day discovering the heart of God for your family, friends, and for yourself, the more attached you will become to caring about Christ in your life.

Knowing changes everything. The more you learn and know about our amazing God, the more passion will arise in you for His cause. At times, we shy away from fervent people, especially if they seem overly passionate. However, passion does not have to be translated into pushiness. It is simply something that drives your motivation. Have you been lacking motivation in life? Then pursue Jesus! In the pursuit of Him, you will find a passion that comes only from Him—a passion for people, your family, and our world. Even your priorities will begin to change because of the zeal you have for Christ. It will evoke an attitude change in you. Life will be driven by something meaningful.

So often our worldly passions drive us to follow things that bring emptiness. Let your pursuit be toward knowing Jesus more. God is alive today just as He was yesterday. Don't allow yourself to get by on an old memory with God. When Jesus begins to speak a living word to you, passion will arise and bring a fulfillment like you have never known. It will change your relationships and the way you function in them. Your role will change from being a problem-solver to being a seeker of the One who solves your problems. You will find yourself doing things differently than before and seeing new results that bring life, peace, and joy, instead of fear, frustration, and confusion. The passion of the world will end up robbing you whereas the passion of God will continuously give back to you so that you never feel empty.

Ask the Holy Spirit to come and ignite your passion for Jesus as you seek Him today. Pray that the Lord would increase your hunger for Him. He is the only one that satisfies.

Passion:
"When Jesus begins to speak a living word to you, your passion will arise and bring a fulfillment like you have never known. It will change your relationships and the way you function in them. Your role will change from being a problem-solver to being a seeker of the One who solves your problems for you. You will find yourself doing things differently than you did them before and seeing new results that bring life, peace, and joy, instead of fear, frustration, and confusion. The passion of the world will end up robbing you whereas the passion of God will give and replenish you so that you never feel empty."

"For the grace of God that brings salvation has appeared to all men. It teaches us to say 'No' to ungodliness and worldly passions, and to live self-controlled upright and godly lives in this present age." Titus 2:11-12

JOURNAL - DAY TEN

Day 11

IDENTITY

Identity is the way you see yourself. It is the way you determine your worth. The Lord identifies you as belonging to Him. You are His possession. He treasures you. He sees characteristics in you that you may or may not yet see in yourself. This is why it is so important to go to Him to understand who you really are.

The Lord is drawing you to Himself for deeper purposes. He created something unique and special in you that no one else possesses. With all your flaws and places you are afraid to fail, He has called you to make a difference for Him. Often, we are so caught up in our shortcomings and broken places that we begin to believe we are not as useful to the Lord as someone else might be. The troubles of this life have made us messy, but our true identity is wrapped up in one thing: our need for Jesus. Who are you? You are a woman deeply in need of the living God. You are a woman rescued from every type of dark place. You are continually being freed day by day, circumstance by circumstance.

The enemy has been hard at work creating a false image of you. It is an image that is both ungodly and unattainable. He wants to tempt you to chase after a fake representation of what you could become. In Jeremiah 10:14 it says, "Everyone is senseless and without knowledge; every goldsmith is shamed by his idols. The images he makes are a fraud; they have no breath in them." The enemy loves to lie to you. He tells you that you do not measure up to the standards of this world. This is a lie. You do measure up!

When we are walking close to Jesus, the false image that the enemy has created crumbles in the presence of God. You will find the truth about who you are in the presence of God—the truth that you are loved, redeemed, forgiven, and chosen by your Savior. Genesis 1:27 says that God created us in His very own image. Your identity should be found in knowing that you share the very image of God—an image that is full of love, grace, power, hope, peace, beauty, and everything that is good under the sun. It is time to trade your man-made, "less than", flawed image and exchange it for the likeness of who Jesus is in you. Search the Bible for the characteristics of God and receive that as His impartation in your own life. God wants to restore your identity so that you are able to recognize who you really are: a beloved creation of God, able to do His good will which produces satisfaction, joy, and contentment.

Today, bring to the Lord your broken identity. Tell Him how you feel about yourself. Ask Him to exchange your insecurity for a knowing confidence of who you really are. Now go and be confident and shame the enemy. God says that the world does not know you; so do not let it define your identity!

Identity:
"It is time to trade your man-made, 'less than', flawed image and exchange it in for the reflection of who Jesus is in you."

"How great is the love the Father has lavished on us, that we should be called children of God! And that is what we are! The reason the world did not know us is that it did not know Him." 1 John 3:1

JOURNAL - DAY ELEVEN

Day 12

WORTH

Worth is an interesting word. Worth speaks of value. When we talk about self-worth, we are referring to whether or not we think we are valuable. Unfortunately, self-worth is often dependent on how much value people find in us. However, if you combine your self-worth with your faith in who Jesus is, then you will know just how valuable you really are. Faith is believing and hoping in who God is and what He has to offer. Faith believes that you are valuable because God has proclaimed that you are His most treasured possession (Deuteronomy 7:6).

1 Peter 1:7 says that our faith is worth more than gold and can be proved genuine. When you give worth to things in your life, it is usually because they produce something good on your behalf. We often refer to things that are worth a lot or speak of opportunities that are worth doing. It is your faith in Jesus that carries more worth than anything else you could pursue. Your faith has a value to the Lord that causes Him to move and work on your behalf. Faith is one of the most valuable assets you possess in your life and produces more than you know. It is of great worth.

If you put your faith and self-worth in Christ above all else, your life will have meaning and regain value. You will begin to see the miracles of God all around you and hunger to see more. Mountains will be moved on your behalf! A spirit of praise will rise up in you and you will begin to see yourself in the light of God's love over your life. As you obey the Lord, you will find that daily life situations will go from dull and mundane to completely worth doing. It is worth it to have faith in God's plan. God thinks you are worth making the plan for!

Worth and faith together make all the difference. When you believe who Jesus is, what He has done for you, and what He wants to do in and through your life, you will find a new kind of significance that motivates you everyday. Suddenly, spending your time, your money, and energy is worth it when you think of what Jesus can do with your life and resources. When you place yourself in the hand of God, He adds power. The Lord demonstrates His amazing works while you have a front row seat. Find your treasure in Christ. Obey Him. You will find that all of this surrender is going to be worth it.

Ask the Lord to show you which things you have placed value and worth in that need to be realigned with your faith in who Jesus is and what He wants to do with your life. Significance and worth are knocking at your door to accompany you on your journey of obedience to God. Today as you empty the dishwasher, ask the Lord to re-prioritize the things you place value in.

Worth:
"If you put your faith and self-worth in Christ above all else, your life will have meaning and regain value."

"Where your treasure is, there your heart will be also." Luke 12:34

JOURNAL - DAY TWELVE

Day 13

LOVE

When thinking about love we often consider it in the context of feelings for others. But much of the time, we are wrapped up in simply loving ourselves. The business of life tends to keep us consumed with an inward focus. However, God's desire is quite the opposite. He asks us to love people around us and to be willing to spend ourselves on them. Afterwards, God replenishes us.

Society teaches you to look out for number one; to work intensely at gaining the best the world has to offer us as an individual. Jesus teaches us to humble ourselves, love others and He will lift us up. We have it backwards in so many areas of our lives. Despite knowing the Lord, we can easily fall into the trap of looking out for our own best interest. We become self-absorbed as we focus inwardly. Inward focus causes us to turn away from living a life of love. When we ask Jesus to grow His perfect love in us, our lives begin to change. Insecurity shrinks down as the Lord's truth saturates our lives. Self-reliance dissolves as we recognize our need for the Lord. Self-absorption is diminished when the Holy Spirit reveals our need for Christ and for each other.

The enemy would love to have you believe that you have life under control. In actuality, the opposite is true. Fear comes when we take control of our own lives. We are susceptible to the lies of the enemy. In this vulnerable place, insecurity, doubt, and depression find their way into our lives bringing defeat and despair. However, 1 John 4:18, talks about perfect love driving fear away. Love is the one thing the enemy has none of! If you function out of God's love, you are moving daily in the opposite spirit of everything the enemy has tried to use to destroy your life. The Lord wants to grow love in your life; love that casts out the ensnaring effects of fear. Fear causes you to draw from the withered root of insecurity. Love allows you to function from the nourishing root of Christ.

Be motivated by love. Love does not equal the ability to be nice once in a while. Love is a powerful gift that only comes from God. It enables you to overcome your natural human response. Ask the Lord to fill you with His love. Love will bring healing to your marriage. As you put others first, ugliness will be revealed and dealt with. Love will bring courage to your life. Invest in seeking God's love—you will receive back more than you ever dreamed of. Love will drive you to pray over people and bring them to the One who can heal, save, and restore. Love will make your life's story magnificent. We must choose love every day.

Ask the Lord to place a perfect love within your heart. Pray that love will be one of your character traits. Ask the Lord for His love to find its way so deep into your core that you begin to function in it as well as live for it. There is nothing greater! Let love permeate every part of you. This happens only by the power of Christ in you. So let Jesus take over today!

Love:
"When we ask Jesus to grow His perfect love in us, our lives begin to change. Insecurity shrinks down as the Lord's truth saturates our lives. Self-reliance dissolves as we recognize our need for the Lord. Self-absorption is diminished when the Holy Spirit reveals our need for Christ and for each other. The life of love is the fulfilling life."

"'Love the Lord your God with all your heart and with all your soul and with all your strength and with all your mind' and 'Love your neighbor as yourself.'" Luke 10:27

JOURNAL - DAY THIRTEEN

Day 14

PURSUIT

When we pursue God, we are taking action on our part to know Him, to listen to His voice, and to enlist ourselves in His service—not just momentarily—but day after day after day. It is difficult to feel like we are pursuing God in the midst of routine. However, pursuing is not an action that requires emotion, it requires obedience.

When you follow something, you move your feet and lift up your head to see where it will go. Your eyes follow the object even when it's on the move. A puppy will pursue a ball not only when it is steady on the ground, but also when it is moving through the air. God is on the move, and every day he longs for us to experience and see what He is doing both in our lives and in the lives of those around us. When we pursue God, our eyes are constantly watching in anticipation for His moving. We actively await His next move, and we are ready to follow.

In Luke 18:43, a man turns to Jesus and asks for healing. It says, "Immediately he received his sight and followed Jesus, praising God. When all the people saw it, they also praised God." When we follow and observe all that God is doing, our response is one of praise and going after. When you are careful to follow and pursue with your eyes what the Lord has set out to do, your heart is filled with praise instead of stress and discouragement. Praise uplifts your spirit. Praise is the act of testifying to God's goodness in both the small and large things.

It is by our testimony that we prove we are watching the Lord. When you speak about the greatness of God, or about what He has done in your life, you demonstrate by your words that you are actively pursuing Him. Are your feet ready to follow where the Lord leads? Are your eyes watching for what He is doing outside the four walls of your home? Is your heart pursuing His truth and discerning His voice? If not, change your posture to the ready position.

As you journal, write down one or two things that you have seen God do in the past year. Then, at some point in the week ahead, share it with someone. This is how you know you are actively following and pursuing the Lord. Get up, keep your eyes on Jesus, speak about His amazing deeds, pursue Him with a sprinting spirit, and be filled with praise!

Ask the Lord to open your eyes to the work He is doing all around you. Ask Jesus to train you to pursue and follow His work above all else. He will grow a new kind of awareness in you that is zealous for the things of God.

Pursuit:
"God is on the move, and every day He longs for us to experience and see what He is doing both in our lives and in the lives of those around us. When we pursue God, our eyes are constantly watching in anticipation for His moving. We actively await His next move, and we are ready to follow."

"For the eyes of the Lord range throughout the earth to strengthen those whose hearts are fully committed to Him." 2 Chronicles 16:9a

JOURNAL - DAY FOURTEEN

Day 15

INSECURITY

Today I hope that you are proud of yourself! You are half-way through your journey of seeking the Lord throughout your daily routine. For some of you, the fruit of this work will come later. You are sowing seeds of dedication and determination that will allow you to see the glory of the Lord even in the monotony of life. He will surprise you with how those seeds grow up to produce a meaningful harvest in your life. So keep it up!

Our word for the day is "insecurity." Even the godliest woman struggles with this because the enemy wants to make her feel defeated and weak in life. Often times we think the root of insecurity is failure and fault but in reality the root of insecurity is self-reliance and pride. Self-reliance gives you an artificial sense that you can control your own life. This kind of pride then produces fear because at some point you will begin to feel that you are losing control. There is a crippling fear and its name is insecurity. It debilitates you, disarms you, and puts you down. Insecurity causes you to look inward and find fault within yourself. The ironic part is, of course, there are faults in us!

It is in the times that we are feeling great that the enemy escorts us to a place of pride. The devil dines with us there and feeds our self-focus. He then gives us the reigns over our life situations and we take them. We feel a false sense of confidence in ourselves and arise and wait for our own applause and self-glorification. Then he leaves us for a moment standing in the midst of our pride. Pride produces self-sufficiency; self-sufficiency produces fear of failure. Fear of failure produces insecurity; insecurity produces inability. It is at this point of recognition that the enemy pulls you down and shows you all your flaws. He reminds you who you really are as a fallen human being and you are left with an abundance of insecurity and anxiety.

We would not be insecure about our flaws and shortcomings if we stayed at the feet of Jesus. We would recognize His voice and the Lord would remind us that He desires to use us even in our weakness. At the feet of Jesus, our limitations just serve as a reminder of His amazing grace and redemption. Our flaws should not cause us to shrink down but rather to rise up in praise to the One who has made us new. 2 Corinthians 12:9-10 says, "But He [The Lord] said to me, 'My grace is sufficient for you, for my power is made perfect in weakness.' Therefore I will boast all the more gladly about my weakness, so that Christ's power may rest on me. That is why, for Christ's sake, I delight in

INSECURITY

my weakness, in insults, in hardship, in persecution, in difficulties. For when I am weak, then I am strong."

When Jesus gives us strength in our shortcomings, we cannot help but praise Him for His miraculous victory in our lives. As we remain in a spirit of humility before the Lord, we find such a sense of security in Him that no matter what our issue, we know that Jesus can take care of it. When our focus is not on our own ability, then insecurity leaves. It is only God who can control and move the pieces of your life according to His goodness.

I want to caution you from my own experience, that if you are in a season of pride and self-reliance, run! You are in the company of a destroyer! Fall on your knees before the King. Do not forget who you really are—a flawed human being in great need of a redeemer. You are sent with His presence to serve Him in wholeness! It is at this place that the Lord will spare you from fear, anxiety, and a sense of insecurity that runs your life and makes you feel useless.

I know that each one of us has struggled with feelings of insecurity at some point in our lives. It may be due to a poor self-image, a lack of love, loss of friendships, or an inattentive spouse. Jesus wants to let you know that if you will surrender control, He will redeem your inadequacies and use them to become your testimony. The Lord will surprise you with His miraculous power despite all of your weaknesses.

Ask Jesus to come and free you from your own fears. Pray that He will help you renew your mind so that you can be freed from a crippling insecurity. Be alert when the enemy whispers lies about who you are and what you are not. Ask the Lord to help you run to truth.

Insecurity:
"When Jesus gives us strength in our shortcomings, we cannot help but praise Him for His miraculous victory in our lives. As we remain in a spirit of humility before the Lord we find such a sense of security in Him that no matter what our issue, we know that Jesus can take care of it."

"But he said to me, 'My grace is sufficient for you, for my power is made perfect in weakness.' Therefore I will boast all the more gladly about my weaknesses, so that Christ's power may rest on me. That is why, for Christ's sake, I delight in weaknesses, in insults, in hardships, in persecutions, in difficulties. For when I am weak, then I am strong." 2 Corinthians 12:9&10

JOURNAL - DAY FIFTEEN

Day 16

HUMILITY

"Clothe yourself with humility toward one another because God opposes the proud but gives grace to the humble. Humble yourself, therefore, under God's mighty hand, that He may lift you up in due time. Cast all your anxiety on Him because He cares for you" (2 Peter 5:5a-7).

Sometimes we view humility like a diet. We think, "If I can suffer in this for a little while longer, then I can go back to what I was doing before and see different results this time." We humble ourselves today, and yet stand in our pride tomorrow. Pride puts us on the throne while humility bows before a loving King. The act of true humility comes from knowing Jesus. True humility comes as a necessity when we have met with the Almighty God. His greatness overwhelms our smallness and we bow in gratitude toward His grace.

Yet even with the knowledge of His power, our hearts are deceitful. Pride and control are the cravings of mankind. When a spirit of pride sets in, it is because we have bought into the lie that we are making it on our own. The truth is, we either make it with God, or we don't make it at all! "For all things were created by Him and for Him" (Colossians 1:16b). Outside of Christ, there is no power to survive. There is no victory that is won. There is no restoration or redemption. There is no good thing that comes without Him.

Humility is the recognition of your unending need for God. It is not some act of lowliness that you have to muster up. It is not pretending that others are so great and that you are not. Humility becomes the natural posture of your heart when you are saturated in the presence of the Lord. 2 Peter 5:7 says, "Cast your anxiety on Him because He cares for you." It does not say "He cares *about* you," although He does. It says, "He cares *for* you." He is your caretaker. He is your refuge and strength. Outside of Him there is no other. Just as I said earlier in this devotion, pride brings self-reliance; self-reliance brings the fear of failure. Fear of failure brings insecurity; insecurity brings inability. When the scripture tells us to cast our anxiety on the Lord, it is teaching us to go back to the root of that anxiety which is pride and self-sufficiency. That is why this scripture continues on humility by saying, "Humble yourself therefore under God's Mighty hand, that He may lift you up in due time. Cast all your anxiety on Him because He cares for you" (1 Peter 5:6-7).

HUMILITY

When you start to spend consistent time in the presence of the Lord, you will find the ability to lay down the right to be in charge of your own life, and recognize that you are desperate for God to be the authority. The Lord also places leaders in your life and asks you to submit to their authority. This takes humility. Humbling yourself to any authority that God has placed in your life is not a subservient role but rather a godly attitude of the heart. He desires to work all things out in you according to His good purpose.

Sometimes we lack humility because we are offended. When we become offended, our pride has been hurt. We need to humble ourselves before the Lord and take our offended pride to the feet of Jesus. Allow Him to help you step down from your wounded platform to receive from Him. Let Him work it out for you. Let His love wash over you. Recognize that apart from Him you can produce nothing that is fruitful. Let Jesus heal your offended heart, my friend.

Jesus says, in Matthew 11:29, "Take my yoke upon you and learn from me, for I am gentle and humble in heart, and you will find rest for your souls." He says, "Learn from me." When you are completely surrendered to the Lord you will find the rest you so desperately need. Humble yourself in the presence of your Jesus. Lift up His name everyday and watch what He will do in and through you.

Come humbly before the Lord your God. Take your wounded pride to Him and ask Him to help you relinquish control. Ask Him to saturate you in His presence. It is at His feet that humility becomes your delight.

Humility:
"Humility is the recognition of your unending need for God. It is not some act of lowliness that you have to muster up. It is not pretending that others are so great and that you are not. Humility comes upon you when you are saturated in the presence of God Almighty."

"Humble yourself in the sight of the Lord and He will lift you up." 2 Peter 5:5

JOURNAL - DAY SIXTEEN

Day 17

PURPOSE

There are many days that go by where the only purpose is just to get things checked off of our lists. On occasion, there are times where the Lord interrupts our routine to impact someone else's life. When He does that, it suddenly feels like we have been filled with a purpose. When purpose accompanies your life, it is as if you have found a treasure that has been buried. When you find that treasure, it causes your spirit to worship and your soul to understand God's divine intervention in your life.

If you are in Christ, you have a purpose to follow Him and to be His witness. This can be accomplished on any given day. It is when we set our mind on pursuing the Lord that the reason for existing changes. You exist to have a personal relationship with God. He is waiting to talk to you everyday so that you can come alive with the significance of His plan instead of simply fulfilling duties.

Purpose is what drives us to do the things we do. We clean our house for the purpose of bringing order, peace, and beauty. We do our hair for the purpose of avoiding embarrassment or to feel good about ourselves. We eat for the purpose of curbing hunger and gaining energy. But what is the purpose or the reason why we serve the Lord? We serve the Lord because we know that He is the only one who can make our lives new. Jesus can redeem any situation and reveal any truth. He can restore the past and bring healing. We live to allow Jesus to surprise us with His goodness and for us to testify of what He has done in return.

It is possible to grow in purpose, but it is a choice. We make a decision every morning to choose either our purpose or the purpose of God. If your purpose for rising is to worship the Lord who brings hope, joy, and peace, then your heart will be satisfied in His will. You will let the Lord into your routine and He will speak to you throughout your day. It is God's desire for you to be aligned with His purpose for living. Look for God's divine intervention in your life.

Pray that the Lord will renew your purpose and allow your heart to come into alignment with His plans for you. Every day can be a day full of purpose if we set our hearts to prayer and to allow God to use our lives to minister to our families, our friends, and to our neighbors. The Lord desires to have all of your heart, all of your mind, and all of your soul. Live with the intent and purpose of listening to the voice of the Lord and being obedient to Him.

Purpose:
"It is possible to grow in purpose, but it is a choice. We make a decision every morning to choose either our purpose or the purpose of God."

"Many are the plans in a man's heart, but it is the LORD's purpose that prevails." Proverbs 19:21

JOURNAL - DAY SEVENTEEN

Day 18

STRENGTH

"As for God, His way is perfect; the word of the Lord is flawless. He is a shield for all who take refuge in Him. For who is God besides the Lord? And who is our Rock except our God? It is God who arms me with strength and makes my way perfect. He makes my feet like the feet of a deer; He enables me to stand on the heights" (2 Samuel 22:31-34).

God is your enabler. When life has you on a rocky plain, God gives you the sure footing needed to stand in unsure places. On this eighteenth day of your journey, declare in your home that there is no one like the Lord. There is no one—not a friend, not a spouse, not a child—and there is nothing that compares with the treasure that God Himself can be in your life. He is your answer to everything. God is more than a relationship; He is all you need and more. God is your strength.

The Word says, "He arms you with strength" (2 Samuel 22:33). When you feel completely incapable of doing it on your own and are worn out, God clothes you with strength that does not originally belong to you. He does not give an extra dose of your own strength or just surge your ability. He arms you with a strength that is outside of you—a strength that originates from Him. It comes from His presence and His ability. We are frail, but God is our place of refuge. The Lord becomes your rock. He changes your mind-set from one of feeling like you are on shaky ground to one of knowing that you are secure with Him. When we say God is our strength, we are admitting we are in need of Him.

In what areas do you need strength today? Is it simply the strength to get through the day? Is it the strength to stand for what is right? Is it the strength to be strong for your marriage? Is it the strength to listen to the voice of the Lord and tune out the lies of the enemy? Whatever it is, the strength will not come from you! Ask the Lord to arm you with His strength and He will show you your vulnerabilities and reveal His sufficiency. If you are holding on in your ability by a thread, let go! Surrender yourself to the Lord. Raise your flag and give up! Let Him come to the rescue and save you. He will then restore and fill you with His own Spirit. He strengthens you as you wait upon Him.

Jesus never grows tired and cannot be weary. You are not a burden to the Lord. He puts you on His wings and lifts you up. Trust Him for He is trustworthy. Surrender to Him! Lay down your life issues and He will pick them up and bring you to victory. The Lord Almighty is your rock and strength.

Ask the Lord to show you the areas in your life where you have relied on your own strength. Ask Jesus to clothe you with His strength instead of your own. Be confident in the power of God in your life.

Strength:
"When you feel completely incapable to do something on your own and are worn out, God clothes you with strength that does not originally belong to you. He does not give you an extra dose of your own strength or just surge your ability. He arms you with a strength that is outside of you—a strength that originates from Him."

"I know what it is to be in need, and I know what it is to have plenty. I have learned the secret of being content in any and every situation, whether well fed or hungry, whether living in plenty or in want. I can do everything through Him who gives me strength." Colossians 4:12&13

JOURNAL - DAY EIGHTEEN

Day 19

PERSEVERANCE

Are you in the midst of what seems like a never-ending battle? Are you crying out, "I give up Lord!"? Are you are afraid to take the next step to which God is calling you? The Bible says, "You need to persevere so that when you have done the will of God you will receive what He has promised" (Hebrews 10:36). God knows there are moments when you feel like quitting. It can be hard to walk in the direction that God is leading us in especially during trials. If you press through, you will receive the promises of God. It does not mean that the path will not be rocky, but that He will give you the perseverance to walk in His will. He is faithful to come through for you!

God gives us friends, accountability partners, as well as the church to help us persevere in this life. When it comes to perseverance, accountability plays such an active role. We need accountability from the smallest matters of life to the most vital. If we have a friend standing in the gap with us giving encouragement, it is easier for us to persevere through our situation and stay on track. It is the Lord's desire that you are persistent in the things that line up with His will for your life. However, He knows that we put ourselves down. He sees the enemy on the prowl trying to destroy you. Persevering is not a simple task! When you are worn out and tired it is easy to give up and to allow the waves of life to crash over you. This is when you must stand up again and find the strength from the Lord to persevere. At the end of your circumstance, you will look back and notice that God was with you all along; taking you farther than you could ever have imagined when your trial first began.

Do you need some encouragement today? Do you need someone to stand beside and help you believe for your marriage? For your weight loss journey? For that unreached goal? I encourage you to tell someone around you what you are trying to accomplish or even stay away from. Allow them to help you and encourage you. Allow your godly friends to speak wisdom into your life and to help you continue on fighting your battles with faith. Perseverance is contagious. When you are running in a race and you begin to tire out, all it takes to continue on is seeing another runner persevering and going on ahead of you. That gives you your second wind and motivates you to press through the pain to finish the race. Look for that other "runner" in your life to help you persevere through your race!

Even in this thirty day journey, don't give up! It may seem that no one in your family has even

PERSEVERANCE

noticed that you have put their clothes away every day and that you have been diligent in praying on their behalf, but I am sending you my encouragement to keep going. God notices what you are doing my friend, and He will honor your commitment to persevere to the end.

James 1:3-4 says, "You know that the testing of your faith develops perseverance. Perseverance must finish its work so that you may be mature and complete, not lacking anything." Perseverance can be developed in your life, but it comes with dedication. Keep praying for that loved one. Keep persevering toward your goals. Keep your chin up, do not lose heart, and run this journey with an accountability partner.

Ask a friend to join you in your determination. Call someone and ask them to pray with you for perseverance. Tell them what you are going through and ask them to keep checking up on you in that area. Ask Jesus to come and fill you with a renewed sense of resolve to see it through. I am cheering you on! Whatever it is, the Lord desires to bring victory to your life.

Perseverance:
"Persevering is not a simple task! When we are worn out and tired it is easy to give up and to allow the waves of life to crash over you. This is when you must stand up again and find the strength from the Lord to persevere."

"As you know, we consider blessed those who have persevered. You have heard of Job's perseverance and have seen what the Lord finally brought about. The Lord is full of compassion and mercy." James 5:11

JOURNAL - DAY NINETEEN

Day 20

WAITING

"I waited patiently for the Lord; He turned to me and heard my cry" (Psalm 40:1).

Nobody likes to wait. It is against our very nature to wait for something. Our society has taught us that when we want something we get it now. We have grown accustomed to modern conveniences and immediate gratification. Unfortunately, this attitude can spill over into our relationship with God. We can slip into a child-like tantrum when we have to wait for God's answers and for His timing.

Children display this need for instant gratification when they whine in the middle of the waiting. We often tell kids, "You're just going to have to wait." Or, "Just wait a minute." Even as adults, waiting does not get any easier. We do not throw ourselves on the floor in a tantrum, but when we have to wait, our heart may feel anxious, frustrated, or tired when the delay seems too long. As grown women we know that there are many things we have to wait for and we have learned to live with that reality. Nevertheless, training our attitude to relax in the "wait" is a skill to be learned.

Have you ever been in the car with kids on a road trip and gotten the question from the backseat over and over again, "Are we there yet?" Have you been saying to God, "Are we there yet?" Is there something that you have been praying for that the Lord has not yet answered? For most of us, the answer to that question is "yes." Perhaps you have waited so long that it feels like God is not listening anymore. Have you felt like His answer was delayed because you were doing something wrong? Does it feel like God is making you wait for no reason? The truth is that waiting is all about the right timing. Psalm 31:15 says, "My times are in His hands." The Lord knows the future. He knows everything about you. He loves you with an everlasting love. He desires to give you good gifts. If it feels like it has been way too long since He has responded to your prayer, it is not because He wants to make you wait simply for the sake of teaching you a lesson. It is not because He is too busy for you.

You are waiting for His perfect timing. Instead of focusing so much on the waiting that comes in between the question and the answer, we must train our spirit to trust His timing. If your child was tired of standing at a cross walk and decided it looked safe to cross, you know that running out at the

WAITING

wrong time could be life-threatening. This is the same with us. If we knew what was coming around the corner, we would not try to overstep the Lord's timing in our lives. We would rejoice in His goodness and trust His love.

God is working out the unknown even when it seems that things in life have come to a halt. Waiting is about trusting God's timing. Do you trust that God hears? Do you trust that He can do anything on your behalf? Do you trust his timing?

Ask the Lord to give you the patience to wait. Be persistent in your prayers knowing that the Lord hears. Remember that the reason you are waiting for an answer is because He is taking care of the timing.

***Waiting*:**
"Waiting is all about trusting God's timing."

"I waited patiently for the Lord; He turned to me and heard my cry." Psalm 40:1

JOURNAL - DAY TWENTY

Day 21

CALLING

Jesus is drawing us to Himself by the calling of His Holy Spirit. The Spirit allows us to know God, to be amazed at what He has done for us, and then to go and share the hope of what He can do for people of all nations. Having a calling on your life does not mean that God is sending you to Africa to be a missionary, although that might be the case. Having the call of God on your life means that He is actively drawing you in to listen intently to His voice and to obey Him.

We are God's creation. Therefore we have an urge within us to follow God's ways and to search for Him. Time after time we have seen people come and search for the Lord without any understanding as to why they are yearning to search for a God that may or may not exist. They do not realize that they are seeking God because He does exist. We were created to pursue Him in our lives. It is the Lord who draws all people to Him. Jesus is calling you. The very spirit that resides in you agrees that following Christ is your destiny! Often times we search for some big calling or spiritual moment with God. The only true calling we need to worry about is the one in which Jesus has called us into a deeper relationship with Him. Do not allow yourself to get caught up in the details of how He will use you to accomplish great things. God can work in your everyday life situations to accomplish more than you know.

Jesus is calling you to His presence and His presence comes anytime and anywhere you invite Him. It is in His presence that we hear His voice and understand His word. When we come close to Him our prayers are heard. "In His presence there is fullness of joy" (Psalm 16:11 NKJV). Being with Jesus is your calling! When God draws you into a deeper relationship with Him, your heart will long to study His word, listen to His voice, and obey His leading. At the moment, He might be calling you to love your kids a little more or to focus on your spouse for the evening. He might ask you to invite your neighbor to your church, or to go on a mission's trip. Calling is not a one-time thing for a particular job in ministry. It is a drawing towards being obedient to Jesus, sitting at His feet and learning from Him. It is in obedience that we find fulfillment in our calling.

Today, Jesus is calling you to spend time with Him. He is calling you to know Him. He is calling you to worship Him and to seek Him. He is calling you to be healed, set free, and filled with hope. So start fulfilling the call of God on your life by abiding in Him.

Ask the Lord to draw you in today—so close that your ears are open to hear what He wants to say to you. Then be obedient and go. Take that leap of faith and simply obey. Listen to His voice, read the word of God, and jump into the great adventure He has for you.

Calling:
"Often times we search for some big calling or spiritual moment with God. The only true calling we need to worry about is the one in which Jesus has called us into a deeper relationship with Him."

"You did not choose me but I chose you and appointed you to go and bear fruit. Fruit that will last."
John 15:16

JOURNAL - DAY TWENTY ONE

Day 22

BELIEF

Mark 9:14-32 tells us that Jesus came to His disciples. He found them arguing with the teachers of the law and asked why they were quarreling. A man from the crowd came forward and told Jesus that he had brought his son whom he believed was possessed by an evil spirit to be healed, but that the disciples could not drive the spirit out. Jesus replied, "Oh you unbelieving generation. How long shall I stay with you?" (v19). The man then brought the boy to Jesus and said, "If you can do anything take pity on us and help." (v22b). "If you can?" Jesus repeats. "Everything is possible for him who believes," (v23) He said. Then Jesus cast the spirit out of the boy and he was freed. The disciples could not cast the evil spirit out of the boy because they did not believe they had power to do so. Yet now we have the privilege of having power. After Jesus ascended to heaven, He sent His Spirit to dwell within the heart of mankind. It is His Spirit that gives power and testifies to God's omnipresence and authority through miraculous deeds. If you have accepted Jesus as your savior, you have His very life and Spirit living in you.

Jesus has the ability to meet you in your need today. He carries all authority over your life and over every circumstance you face. The question is: Do you believe He can?

If God lives in us we have access to the power of Christ at any moment. I think the Lord would ask us once again, "Do you believe?" The disciples knew Jesus was near; they knew He had the power to heal the boy. Still, they were not quite sure what to do. Often, we come to Jesus, like the man with the boy, and say, "If you can do anything take pity on me." It is our unbelief that causes us to be timid in asking and preempt our question to God with, "If you can," when we should already know the answer: Yes He can! Let those three words resonate in your spirit today. Bring those three words into alignment with the current situation you are struggling with. Declare, "Yes He can!"

Maybe you still need convincing. Throughout scripture, Jesus shows us the evidence of His ability and power. God still holds the power to do the miraculous in your life today. We can be confident that God will work in our situation. If you've been in the same struggle for longer than you like, it doesn't mean God cannot or does not want to help. He is at work on your behalf—some work just takes longer. God is faithful to bring comfort and to bring about our personal change in the process. Let your belief in Jesus meet up with your desire to be changed by Him today.

Ask the Lord to deliver you from unbelief. Ask Him to deposit in you an unwavering hope that gives you patience and understanding in the waiting. God is on the move. He never sleeps. He never quits. Let's be the believing generation that allows the Lord to do His work and trusts that He is doing it in accordance with His perfect timing and power.

Belief:
"It is our unbelief that causes us to be timid in our asking and preempt our question to God with, 'If you can,' when we should already know the answer: Yes He can! Let those three words resonate in your spirit today."

"Then Jesus said to Thomas, 'Put your finger here; see My hands. Reach out your hand and put it in My side. Stop doubting and believe. Thomas said to Him, 'My Lord and My God!' Then Jesus told him, 'Because you have seen Me, you have believed; but blessed are those who have not seen and yet have believed.'" John 20:27-29

JOURNAL - DAY TWENTY TWO

Day 23

TRUST

Faith begins when we first believe in the name of Jesus, but trust comes when we build our relationship with Him. Trust requires an understanding of who God is. Trust requires a confidence in God's character. So the best way to build trust in God is by spending time with the Lord. As we develop a daily relationship with Christ, we will begin to see His character prove itself over and over again. That is when trust changes from being something you desire to something you actually have.

When life throws itself at you like a hurricane, your trust is tested. Your trust system is sifted when you are in the middle of the trial and faced with the question, "Are you, in this very moment, able to function with peace because you really do believe God is in control?" It is easy to say we trust the Lord, but until we take steps of obedience to jump into the unknown and believe He will prove faithful, we have not actually tested our trust system. Trust is more than a belief; it is an action.

"Trust in the Lord with all your heart and lean not on your own understanding. In all your ways acknowledge Him and He will make your paths straight" (Proverbs 3:5-6). This verse tells us that our hearts must choose to trust and believe the character and truths of God. After we actually take the action to walk in that knowledge, He then promises to direct us. Perhaps you have said that you trust Jesus but have had a difficult time transferring your words into action. The Lord is saying to you, take the leap of faith and trust His leading.

When you feel the prompting of His Spirit, believe what He has for you, and put aside worry and doubt. Practice giving up control and trust in the ability of God. While reading His word, let it bring conviction to the areas in life that you need to release control of. For example, if the Lord tells you to go to a stranger and pray for them, do just that! Step out and trust that God will be faithful and go pray for them. Start putting action into your trust system and strengthen your faith by being obedient. He will astound you with how He will come through for you!

You can trust the Lord. When you step out in faith, He will catch you! He is faithful. He is all that He says He is. He will never fail. There is no fault or wrong in Him. The Lord Almighty is sovereign. He sees your whole life. He desires what is best for you and He has the ability to keep you from all harm. Act out your trust today and tell one of your friends how you did that!

Ask the Lord to heal your mistrust. Pray for the courage to add action to your trust. Proclaim the trustworthiness of God today.

Trust:
"Trust requires an understanding of who God is. Trust requires a confidence in God's character. So the best way to build your trust is to spend time with the Lord. When you have a daily relationship with Christ you will begin to see His character prove itself over and over again. That is when trust changes from being something you desire to something you actually have."

"Many are the woes of the wicked, but the Lord's unfailing love surrounds the {woman} who trusts in Him." Psalm 32:10

JOURNAL - DAY TWENTY THREE

Day 24

ANGER

Anger is the emotion that comes when you have been offended, wronged, denied, or taken from. It can be dangerous when your anger conspires within you to undo that offense through retaliation.

Nobody likes to feel angry. It stews in your stomach and gives ache to your heart. Anger can be like poison. When you drink it in, it kills from the inside out. It could be several times a week, or even every day, that somebody annoys you, offends you, or wrongs you. It might even feel like you have the right to take up an attitude of anger toward them.

Anger makes you feel like you have power, but it actually disarms you. In fact, many times anger can take away your effectiveness and just drive you further away from your relationships. Anger manifests itself in two ways: first through the feeling that comes upon you when you have been wronged and second through the action that comes when you try to undo that wrong.

The action of anger only transpires after the feeling of anger has convinced you that retaliation is your only solution. If we would train ourselves to go to the Lord in prayer and take our anger to Him, He would free us from the false assumption that the action of anger would do something to right the wrong. Anger makes nothing right. It only fuels your emotion and gives you a false sense of control. It causes you to be irrational and destructive in your behavior. Anger usually results in regret. A word spoken in anger or a reaction lived out of bitterness, can leave scars that take years to heal.

God has the power to silence the anger in your soul. When you feel anger arising, call on the power of God. Ask Him for help. Ask Him for understanding in your offense. Proverbs 14:29 says, "A patient man has great understanding but a quick tempered man displays folly." Patience and understanding are hard to find when you have been wronged. That is why we need the Holy Spirit to fill our hearts with something we do not possess on our own. Go to Jesus. He can help you sift through your emotions and find the truth about your offenses.

I need to derail from this thought process for a moment to say that if you are angry because you are

ANGER

being physically harmed in the situation you are in, then patience is not what you need. You need courage to get out of that situation right away and to get help. The Lord is your protector and does not want you to live in harm! So if this is your situation, find someone to talk to. Then when you have reached a place of safety, take up your shield of faith and the sword of the Spirit, which is the word of God, and ask the Lord to take up His vengeance on your behalf. "Vengeance is Mine," declares the Lord, 'I will repay.' The Lord will judge His people. It is terrifying to fall into the hands of the living God." (Hebrews 10:30-31).

No matter where you find yourself, God will fight on your behalf. When anger arises, go to God. No matter what the case, the Lord wants to train you to stop before you react and to ask Him to reveal truth to you. Ask Him to give you the power to refuse retaliation and to walk in a spirit of grace. The Lord your God is able to redeem all situations. He hears your cry. He knows your need. He sees your offended heart and He wants to help you heal. Today, ask the Lord to show you the areas of your life where anger resides. Maybe it is an old place of offense that you need to let go of. Maybe you have been avoiding a relationship because you have been wronged. Ask the Lord to redeem that friendship or even that marriage. Lay down your offended heart at the cross and ask Jesus to give you the power to forgive. Ask Him for wisdom to know where to start in that broken relationship. Go and ask forgiveness from the person you have been angry with. I am praying that the Lord will fill your heart with peace and self-control as you allow God to take up your cause instead of taking matters into your hands.

Ask the Lord to take control of the anger you are holding. Release your offense to Him and be freed.

Anger:
"A word spoken in anger or a reaction lived out of bitterness can leave scars that take years to heal. God has the power to silence the power of anger in your soul."

"A man's wisdom gives him patience; it is to his glory to overlook an offense."
Proverbs 19:11

JOURNAL - DAY TWENTY FOUR

Day 25

LONELINESS

It is easy to say, "The Lord is with you," but harder to believe when you feel lonely. God designed us to connect with other people. But many times, because of our own assumptions, we keep ourselves closed in. We assume people are too busy to come over or that they already have a lot of friends. We assume they do not want to hear about our trouble. This is not the truth. It is the tactic of the enemy to make you assume that others do not have time for you. The truth is they do have time for you.

One of the best cures for loneliness is courage. If you reach out to another person, even when you are the one who needs the "reaching", that is when you are victorious over loneliness. You have got to take steps to love somebody. The enemy would like to keep you isolated. He wants to whisper into your ear and tell you that you are "less than," that you are unloved, and that you do not fit in. Do not listen to these lies. Do not assume that they are true. When you listen to Jesus and allow His Spirit to speak truth to your mind, you no longer feel like second best.

Jesus wants to free you from a life of loneliness! Loneliness is the daughter of self-pity and self-pity is the enemy of friendship. When you dwell in a place of self-pity, you shut others out. It wraps itself around you in a false sense of comfort and causes you to turn inward. You deny that you even need people in your life who are outside of your immediate family. You cling to your spouse or to your parents to cover up for the loss of relationship. This causes codependency because now you depend on them to sooth your loneliness. It is time to branch out, to reach out, and to live out your courage.

If you will be a good listener to others, if you will ask them questions instead of just assuming how they feel, then you will be well on the road to defeating loneliness in your life. Today is your day to take off the cloak of self-pity and invite yourself to the party of life where you belong! You've got a personal invitation from Jesus! Take steps today to reach out to someone. Do as 1 John 4:18 says and let love cast out your fear.

Pray that the Lord would help you care about somebody else today. You might just be their answer to prayer.

Loneliness:
"Jesus wants to free us from a life of loneliness. Loneliness is the daughter of self-pity and self-pity is the enemy of friendship. When we dwell in a place of self-pity, we shut others out."

"A friend loves at all times." Proverbs 17:17a.

JOURNAL - DAY TWENTY FIVE

Day 26

HOLINESS

Have you ever felt that holiness was unattainable? Does it seem like holiness is a characteristic reserved for Old Testament leaders? When we think of a holy person, we usually imagine someone with a stuffy life or a person who never lives adventurously. This is a false perception of holiness. There is nothing more adventurous than living a life that is holy unto God. This is the life to which the Lord has called each one of us to. His words says, "You shall be holy unto me, for I, the Lord, am holy, and have set you apart from the peoples, that you should be Mine" (Leviticus 20:26).

Pay close attention to what the Bible says concerning holiness. "Therefore gird up the loins of your mind, be sober, and rest your hope fully upon the grace that is to be brought to you at the revelation of Jesus Christ; as obedient children, not conforming yourselves to the former lusts in your ignorance; *but as He who called you is Holy, you also become Holy in all conduct,* because it is written, *'Be Holy, because I am Holy.'* And if you call on the Father, who without partiality judges according to each one's work, behave yourselves throughout the time of your sojourning in fear; knowing that you were not redeemed with corruptible things, like silver or gold, from your vain way of life received by tradition from your fathers, but with the precious blood of Christ, as of a lamb without blemish and without spot" (1Peter 1:13-19 NKJV).

Holiness is not only attainable in our generation; it is required! It is set upon those who bear the name of Christ. One reason we struggle with the word "holiness" is because we are afraid that we will have to give up some of the "fun." When we are holy, we are living against the norm. We are bucking the status quo. It is never boring to live a life that is set apart for God. In fact, there is nothing more satisfying!

The words "holy" and "sanctify" are often interpreted to mean "righteous" or "pure." But the basic concept of the Hebrew word "*qadosh*," or "holiness" as we know it in the English language, is that of apartness and distinction. When you live a life that is set apart for God, the enemy is defeated. Satan cannot cross into holiness. He has been banished from the presence of God and therefore cannot dwell in the holy place. As Christians, we should not dwell in places where the enemy resides. Jesus desires to help you overcome the entrapments of the devourer by living holy and set apart in Christ. When you are able to arm yourself with the truths of God, when you believe that anything

HOLINESS

outside of God's provision brings destruction, then not only will you embrace holiness, you will desire it and will run to it at every turn. Holiness is the power of Christ in you to deny your sinful nature and cling to your new life in Christ. Allow your thoughts to dwell upon the Lord. Let Him steer and guide you. Let Him direct your path and make it straight.

God is calling you to a higher standard. He is calling you to be set apart with Him—to be distinctively marked by the name of Jesus and not by your flesh. Our lives are changed when Christ dwells within us. We are drawn to holiness when we remember that it protects, uplifts, and satisfies. If your life lacks the representation of being set apart for the Lord, then ask Him to come into your stubborn, willful places and show you the destruction that resides when holiness is not present. You become holy when Jesus takes over; for He is holy and He cannot separate Himself from holiness.

Bow your knee today and repent. Holiness is your only way out of destruction. It is also the most courageous way you can live. You will find that being set apart with Jesus will fulfill your life and increase your influence in this day and age. Pray that the Lord will restore holiness in your life.

Holiness:
"When we think of a holy person, we usually imagine someone who has a stuffy life and never lives any adventures. This is a false perception of holiness. There is nothing more adventurous than living a life that is holy. This is the life that God has called each one of us to."

"Make every effort to live in peace with all men and to be holy; without holiness not one will see the Lord." Hebrews 12:14

JOURNAL - DAY TWENTY SIX

Day 27

FEAR

There are two kinds of fear: Fear that brings bondage, and fear that brings life. The fear that cripples you is birthed by the enemy. The fear that sets you free is brought by understanding the love and authority of God. We have a need to fear the Lord. The Lord is mighty to save. He has authority over every stronghold. He drives away the twisted fear brought to you by the enemy. It is to your great benefit to fear the Lord your God.

However, if we choose to ignore the power of Christ in our lives and take back the control and trust in our own ability, then fear will overcome us at every turn. The fear of this world will grip our hearts rendering us defenseless. I cannot express to you the importance of getting to know God and to believe that He holds all authority. When we see God for who He is, then every dark place, every obstacle, every fearful thought within, will be driven away. 1 John 4:18 says, "There is no fear in love. But perfect love drives out fear, because fear has to do with punishment. The one who fears is not made perfect in love." When we stay close to the Lord and hide in the shadow of His protecting wing, we will no longer dwell in the fear that the enemy inflicts, but rather abide in a holy fear toward our loving God.

So, why do we continually live in the company of our fears? It is because we have disarmed ourselves by relying on our own strength to rationalize that fear away! The fear doesn't leave though. We fear the future, we fear for our safety and the safety of our children, we fear disaster, and we fear the dark. We fear rejection; we fear loss. We fear ourselves and we fear the devil. But where is the fear of the Lord our God? The devil certainly fears Him because He knows what God is capable of! So why don't we?

There is only one replacement for the harassing fear in your life. It is learning to fear the Lord instead. The reason we fear God is because He is the "I AM." He carries all authority and is all-powerful. He is the great judge that banished the devil to hell because of the enemy's consuming pride. The Lord sent Himself to reconcile us to Him. He is the way-maker. He can do all things; He can deliver, redeem, cast out, anoint, protect, and be the victor over any life. Do you believe this? Do you hold this truth so close that it makes you stand in a fearful awe of what He will do? If we could grasp just an ounce of who God is, we would tremble and fall on our knees. We would live holy and

FEAR

upright and set ourselves apart with Him. There is no other place of safety except to hide behind His robe. There is no other place to go for salvation. He has the final word and has already won the victory for you. It is simply a matter of you walking the journey to know Him and see the victory first hand. There is only one solution to casting out the fear in our lives, and that is by letting God take over.

The enemy loves to hit us hard when the deep issues of life come our way: divorce, the death of a child, a terrifying experience, a trauma from childhood, a victimizing memory, the loss of your income, the frailty of your life. He pretends to help you arm yourself. He gives you a plastic shield and makes you cower in the corner and shut your eyes just waiting for the horror to pass you by. We stay in that corner and pray for God to deliver us. Stop cowering in the corner! Get up! Run to God who holds the power! Be in awe of His authority over every situation in your life. Give up your insecure, naked fear. Hide behind the Name of the Lord. Revere Him in His power. Take comfort for the Lord your God is to be feared by the enemy. Proverbs 18:10 declares, "The Name of the Lord is a strong tower; the righteous runs into it and are safe." Ask the Lord to exchange your unhealthy fear for a revelation of who He is. Speak the names of Jesus over the fearful, worrisome places in your life. For He is: Emmanuel—God with us, He is All Mighty, Faithful, Savior, Friend, Victor, and the All Powerful One. Fear the Lord for He is mighty to save!

Today, join me in this prayer, "Lord, forgive me for not trusting Your character. Develop the fear of the Lord in me so that I can hide within Your shelter. Lord, You say to earthly fear, 'Go.' And it must leave. So I surrender every fearful thought brought to me by the enemy and I allow You to fight this battle for me. You are victorious over all things! Amen!"

Fear:
"There is only one exchange for the harassing fear in your life, and it is learning to fear the Lord instead."

"I sought the Lord and He answered me; He delivered me from all my fears." Psalm 34:4

JOURNAL - DAY TWENTY SEVEN

Day 28

GRATITUDE

Gratitude is the act of being thankful. It is not merely expressing words; it is also a feeling that rises in you that cannot be pressed down. Gratitude is created when we are truly thankful for what we have or what someone has done for us. You can't hide gratitude. It overflows out of your heart. So why don't we feel grateful all the time? Are we forgetful or taking things for granted?

Time and time again throughout the Bible, it tells us to remember what the Lord has done. Can you think of a time this past week where the Lord met a need in your life? Do you remember when He sent someone to care for you or pray with you? Do not forget about the goodness of God! Train your heart to think about Him. Remember, He resides in the big and little things of life. Wake up in the morning and thank the Lord for the life He has given you. We need to teach our minds to think upon the kindness of God. It says in Philippians 4:8, "Whatever is true, whatever is noble, whatever is right, whatever is pure, whatever is lovely, whatever is admirable – if anything is excellent or praise-worthy – think about such things."

Create a habit of remembering everything the Lord is doing on your behalf. Write it down. Tell it to others. Think about how your path could have changed directions had the Lord not intervened. If you never called upon the name of Jesus to help in your time of need, how would your relationships, self-worth, money, sanity, and peace have turned out? Now, think about the things that have been gained because of Christ: forgiveness, reconciliation, wisdom, friendship, compassion, influence, blessing, peace of mind, a testimony, a home, job, or family. All of these things come from the hand of the Lord! As it is written, "Don't be deceived, my dear brothers. Every good and perfect gift is from above, coming down from the Father of the heavenly lights, who does not change like shifting shadows" (James 1:16-17). Jesus is the giver of all good things! We have so much to be thankful for, but until the thankfulness finds its way into our soul we will not function out of gratitude.

You can train yourself to see the goodness of God by remembering what He has done for you and by opening your eyes to see how He is working in your daily life. Be specific in your thankfulness toward God. Tell the Lord why you are grateful. Thankfulness will find its way into your spirit and you will have no other choice than to spill over with gratitude to the Lord.

Pray that God would remind you of all that Jesus has done in your life. Speak a word of thanks to the Lord throughout your day. Be specific.

***Gratitude*:**
"You can train yourself to see the goodness of God by remembering what He has done for you and by opening your eyes to see how He is working in your daily life."

"Be joyful always; pray continually; give thanks in all circumstances, for this is God's will for you in Christ Jesus." 1 Thessalonians 5:16-18

JOURNAL - DAY TWENTY EIGHT

Day 29

CHANGE

The answer to your freedom is more of Jesus. More of sitting at His feet, more of listening to His voice, more obeying Him, more surrendering, more holy fear of Him, more soaking up His amazing presence. Simply more of Jesus. After going through this study, are you ready for the Lord to change you? Have you been stubborn in your ways?

Too many times we get fat on the word of God, but never exercise its truths. We do Bible studies. We listen to church sermons and shout "Amen!" with whole-hearted agreement, but then we live our lives still burdened by all of the same issues and baggage from the past. It is time to let the Lord set you free from your old way of living. You know what to do, now it is time do it! Let Jesus in everyday. Allow Him to be Lord. Be honest with yourself and with Him. The Lord will be faithful to set you free when you spend time hearing His voice.

I am so proud of you for making it to day twenty nine of this journey. I hope that He has spoken a life changing word into your heart. Perhaps He is giving you the discipline to press into Him more often. Maybe He is fueling your passion to get out of your comfort zone and obey Him fully. Or perhaps He is teaching you to surrender control to Him.

Romans 8:5-8 says, "Those who live according to the sinful nature have their minds set on what that nature desires; but those who live in accordance with the Spirit have their minds set on what the Spirit desires. The mind of sinful man is death, but the mind controlled by the Spirit is life and peace; the sinful mind is hostile to God. It does not submit to God's law, nor can it do so. Those controlled by the sinful nature cannot please God."

It may feel like an impossibility to release your whole life to the Lord and to live upright in everything you do. The truth is, it is impossible! That is the miracle of God's Spirit. It is God who will change you. All you have to do is open your heart. Let the living word of God speak to you. He is a personal God who knows everything that is going on. If you allow Him, He will change you from the inside out by the power of the Holy Spirit.

CHANGE

It is a little like going in for surgery. We would not go in for heart surgery and try to do the work ourselves. We let the skilled surgeon do the job. All we have to do is show up. This is how God is; He is our doctor! If you come, He will repair and restore. Ask the Holy Spirit to show you the areas of your life where you have been stubborn. Ask the Lord to help you let go of the destructive patterns that you have been living in. Come to Jesus and allow amazing change to begin.

Remember what the Lord has spoken during your thirty day journey. Ask him to change you so that you will be ready to take the leap of faith. Let go of your own will and follow His. He will not disappoint you!

***Change*:**
"If you allow Him, He will change you from the inside out by the power of the Holy Spirit."

"Let the wicked change their ways and banish the very thought of doing wrong. Let them turn to the Lord that He may have mercy on them. Yes turn to our God for He will forgive generously." Isaiah 55:7

JOURNAL - DAY TWENTY NINE

Day 30

PRAISE

Praise is the act of lifting up the name of Jesus. It is honoring Him. Adoring Him. Recognizing Him as King. Praise can happen at any moment. You can lift Jesus up in the midst of your stress and turmoil. Something happens in the spiritual realm when you worship the Lord. Praise is the one thing that the enemy cannot use against you. The praise goes from your heart straight to God. When you are in the midst of trouble and you choose to lift up the name of Jesus, the enemy cowers and trembles. When Jesus is lifted up, the enemy loses power over your life. He cannot defeat a woman who praises the Lord!

Do you need a little more praise to come from your life? I know I do! Even in our brokenness and struggles, we can declare the sovereignty of God. By recognizing His position, our faith is strengthened and our circumstance is seen in the light of who God really is. What has been going on in your life over these past thirty days? Perhaps the Lord has brought some things to light that need His healing. He could be showing you some areas where you need the Holy Spirit to come in and change you. Whatever it may be, now is the time to worship the Lord. You need to fall on your face and proclaim that He is the Name above every name, and that there is no person, no other god, under the heavens who can come to your rescue and fulfill your life. It is only Jesus!

So, how do we begin that process of change? To put it simply, change happens when we are on our knees. It happens when we praise and lift up the name of the Lord. Our faith is strengthened and mountains are moved when we bow our knee at the throne of God. Can you imagine the greatness of God? Or has He been diminished in your life? Has He become just another resource that you can go to sometimes? He is not *a* resource. He is *the* source. He is your life. He is your place of comfort. He is the truth. Exalt the name of Jesus over every circumstance in your life. Praise His holy name. There is none like the Lord. Isaiah had a vision and said, "I saw the Lord sitting upon a throne, high and lifted up; and the train of His robe filled the temple" (Isaiah 6:1). The Lord is to be exalted. He rules the whole earth. He is King over all the heavens and He will have the final say over your life.

When you become a woman of praise, your spirit, soul, and mind will follow. Fear must leave in the presence of God. Your faith has sight to see when the Lord is near. Your broken heart is mended when the power of Jesus falls upon you. Worship. Worship. Worship the Lord. He alone is worthy.

PRAISE

Let your heart break open before Him. Even in your kitchen and in your living room, let the praise of the Lord be heard. In front of your children and husband, let the praises of God come out. Let your heart resonate with 1 Chronicles 16:23-31. Say it aloud:

"Sing to the LORD, all the earth;
Proclaim His salvation day after day.
Declare His glory among the nations,
His marvelous deeds among all peoples.
For great is the LORD and most worthy of praise;
He is to be feared above all gods.
For all the gods of the nations are idols,
But the LORD made the heavens.
Splendor and majesty are before Him;
Strength and joy in His dwelling place.
Ascribe to the LORD, O families of nations,
Ascribe to the LORD glory and strength,
Ascribe to the LORD the glory due His name.
Bring an offering and come before Him;
Worship the LORD in the splendor of His Holiness.
Tremble before Him, all the earth!
The world is firmly established; it cannot be moved.
Let the heavens rejoice, let the earth be glad;
Let them say among the nations, "The LORD reigns!"

PRAISE

Praising the Lord is how you reset your life and get your motivation back. Worshipping and glorifying Jesus is how you get out of that rut you are stuck in. In your praises, depression leaves and you become a woman of influence. When you become a woman of praise, you find your courage in the Lord. Let your selfish will bow its knee to the Lord and He will use your life and fill you with joy, purpose, and passion like you have never known.

Worship the Lord with your words of adoration. Pray a prayer of thanks and praise for who He is and what He has begun in your life. Ask Him to reset your mind, soul, and spirit so that you will be renewed, strengthened, and alive in the name of Jesus.

Praise:
"Even in our brokenness and struggles, we can declare the sovereignty of God."

"I will sing of your love and justice; to you, O LORD, I will sing praise." Psalm 101:1

JOURNAL - DAY THIRTY

FINAL TASK

Congratulations! Can you believe you have made it to the end? On day one, you may have thought you would never reach this day, but you, my friend, persevered through. Look back at your thirty day journey and reflect on all that God has spoken to you. Take that wisdom and pursue Him like never before!

Now that you have reached the finish line, it is time to celebrate together and share what the Lord has done. Talk to your facilitator about having a celebration dinner in one of your homes. Take communion together and ask the Lord to do a new work in you. Pray for one another that every area of your lives would come under the submission of Christ and fuel your faith, deepen your friendships, and renew your focus.

In light of what Jesus has done in your life, take some time to write your thirty day story on the next page. I would love to hear the story of how God has restored and created in you a new hunger for seeking Him. If you feel led, please send your story to:

lovingtheleapministries@gmail.com

Your thirty day journey is over but your real journey has just begun. It is God's promise to meet you when you show up at His feet. Be blessed in His presence and seek Him with a renewed passion.

MY THIRTY DAY STORY

When I look back at the last thirty days this is what God spoke to me:

CALENDAR

SUN	MON	TUES	WED	THUR	FRI	SAT

CELEBRATION DINNER:

Date: _____ Time: _____

CONTACT INFORMATION FOR MEMBERS OF MY GROUP

PRAYER REQUESTS

PRAYER REQUESTS

PRAYER REQUESTS

PRAYER REQUESTS

ALL PROFITS GO TO THE WIDOWS & ORPHANS OF AFRICA

World C.O.M.P. reaches out to feed, give medical relief, and bless the poorest of the poor in the slums of Kenya, Africa. They take care of orphans and widows through their feeding centers and micro finance organization. World C.O.M.P. has also ministered to hundreds of boys in the Kenya detention center with the message and love of Jesus Christ. They continue to hold yearly medical camps that minister to thousands of the sick and dying. Their mission is to be a catalyst to inspire, train, and equip Kenyan people to solve some of the largest issues that Kenyans face.

WORLD C.O.M.P stands for "Cry Of My People". This Christian relief organization was founded by Rebekah Metteer's parents, Richard and Valerie Vicknair. Today, the Lord has heard the cry of His people!

Their volunteers transport, cook and serve meals to hundreds of children every day. After lunch, these poverty stricken children are taught basic literacy: reading, writing, and math. World C.O.M.P. also helps HIV and AIDS infected families in the Nairobi Slums.

Their DANSO (Dandori Aids Network Support Organization) has established a Christian community within the slums to help individuals and families affected by HIV and AIDS. Community members help in many practical ways: testing, treatment, dietary essentials, food, childcare, community support and business development through their DANSO microfinance fund.

World C.O.M.P. is also helping hundreds of widows become self-reliant through microfinance. They have established three Microfinance Funds to help widows establish businesses to support their families. Participants receive business counseling, ongoing advice, and accountability to maximize their long-term success.

The organization also ministers in the Shikusa Boys Detention Center. These boys, 13-18 years of age, live on a work farm. Before World C.O.M.P. came, the Center was like a forced labor camp. The boys were in rags, living in fear in a hopeless abusive environment. Their health was very poor and many died during their stay at Shikusa. Through the tireless efforts of World C.O.M.P. board member, Dr. George Matimbai, there has been amazing transformation in this place. The boys are now well fed, the Detention Center Staff have virtually all come to Christ, and most of the boys have accepted Christ! They have provided supplies for vocational training and sports activities. Under the name of "Mercy Ministries" Dr. George is now building a medical clinic on site and dreaming of halfway houses and work internships for them, so when the boys get out they will have a place to go.

If you would like further information on how to partner in prayer and financial support with World C.O.M.P. Relief, you can visit their web site at: www.worldcompkenya.com or by contacting them at:

WorldCOMP
7758 Earl Ave NW
Seattle, WA 98117
(206) 794-5354

ABOUT THE AUTHOR

Rebekah Metteer was born in Seattle, WA. She grew up as a pastor's daughter and has served Jesus from a very young age. Rebekah felt called to ministry in High School while she traveled around the globe to Russia and Korea with a music ministry group. After graduating from Kings High School in Shoreline, WA, Rebekah moved to England to attend a one-year Bible College. It was there that she began to sense a more focused calling on her life to minister to women. Upon graduating from Northwest University with a BA in English and Writing, she began serving at her church in worship and in women's ministry.

Rebekah met her husband Dan at Northwest University in Kirkland, WA and married in 2000. Together they have served in Children's Ministry for the past 11 years. Currently they serve on the Pastoral Staff at Eastridge Church in Issaquah, WA under the quality leadership of Pastor Steve and Cheryl Jamison. She and Dan have three children – Julia, Katie, and Andrew and reside in Snoqualmie, Washington.

When Rebekah is not speaking she loves to camp, sing, decorate and find hidden treasures at thrift stores. Rebekah has become a motivational speaker who delights in seeing women discover who they really are in Christ. Her passion is to see people find such a strong Christ-centered identity that they begin to live in the freedom that God has intended for them. Rebekah lives by the motto, "If I relinquish control to Jesus, he will give back to me the adventure of a life time."

For the past seven years Rebekah has been speaking at women's retreats and young women's events. Along with speaking, she has begun "Loving the Leap Ministries"—a para-church ministry to women to help them set aside the fear, and with great trust in the Lord, to leap into all that God has for them in this amazing adventure called life.

"Loving the Leap Ministries" is also partnering with World COMP relief, led by her parents Richard and Valerie Vicknair, to help support, feed, and dig wells for orphans and widows in the slums of Africa. When Rebekah was a young girl she lived in Kenya while her parents served as missionaries in the Assembly of God. Because of this experience, Rebekah has a special place in her heart to support Kenyans who are in need.

100% of the profits from the sale of this book will go directly to help with micro-financing for African widows and to feeding the orphans there.